NONE
DARE
CALL
IT
TREASON!

BOOK 11

Treasonous
Trade With & Aid To
Enemies Of Freedom!

Robert W. Pelton
$4.95

"Treason doth never prosper,

"What's the reason?

"Why if it prosper,

"None dare call it treason."

John Harrington

Printed in America
On Recycled Paper
In
Charleston, South Carolina

Published in America
By
The Freedom & Liberty
Foundation Press
Knoxville, Tennessee

Dedicated
To

The greatest, most generous, most benevolent and most powerful nation on the face of the earth – and the only country in the history of the world to have been founded on Biblical principles.

A nation can survive its fools, and even the ambitious. But it cannot survive treason from within.

An enemy at the gates is less formidable, for he is known and he carries his banners openly.

The traitor moves among those within the gates freely, his sly whispers rustling through the galleys, heard in the very hall of government itself.

For the traitor appears not traitor. He speaks in the accent familiar to his victims, and he wears their face and their garments, and he appeals to the baseness that lies deep in the hearts of all men.

He rots the soul of a nation - he works secretly and unknown in the night to undermine the pillars of a city - he infects the body politic so that it can no longer resist.

A murderer is less to be feared.

Cicero, 42 B.C.

CONTENTS

Forward

![Independence Hall]

Independence Hall Where the Declaration of Independence Was Signed.

Our glorious Declaration of Independence is a timeless divinely inspired masterpiece given to mankind through the anointed pen of Thomas Jefferson.

The grand and unmatched United States Constitution is indisputably the product of Providential guidance and wisdom and certainly not a document which evokes

13

whimsical interpretations with the changing political climates.

All Americans have a moral obligation to stand up and be counted in these trying times!

Abraham Lincoln boldly declared: *"To sin by silence when they should protest, makes cowards of men."*

William Lloyd Garrison capsulized it best: *"As a free man who is determined to remain free -- I do not wish to think or speak, or write with moderation. "Tell a man whose house is on fire to give a moderate alarm; tell him to moderately rescue his wife from the hands of a ravisher; tell the mother to gradually extricate her babe from the fire into which it has fallen -- but urge me not to use moderation in a course like the present."*

Senator Barry Goldwater, 1964 Presidential candidate was castigated and verbally crucified by the media.

14

He simply stated this simple truism: *"Extremism in the pursuit of Liberty is no vice."*

This good and moral man of character soundly rocked the boat of the propagandists. He was as a result soundly defeated in the election.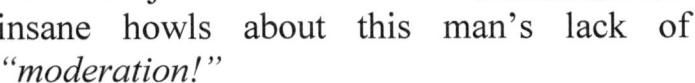

The alarmed media wolves panicked the voters with their jeers and sneers and insane howls about this man's lack of *"moderation!"*

It can honestly be said that through the Providential genius of our Founding Fathers, the remaining remnants of the original American Constitutional Republic still provides more freedom, opportunity and abundance for mankind than is found in any other nation in the world.

This is true despite decade after decade of unabated treason and treachery promulgated by innumerable traitorous individuals found buried in the twiddle dee – twiddle dum administrations of both the Democrats and the Republicans.

 An informed and active, not a media brainwashed electorate, is the only antidote to further prostitution of, and the ultimate destruction of, what Benjamin Franklin called our Republic.

Preface

"Treason against the United States shall consist only in levying war against them, or in adhering to their enemies, giving them aid and comfort."

U.S. Constitution. Article 111, Section 3

What is your treason I.Q.?

If you can answer the following questions, it's high.

If you miss one or more, you should read the *None Dare Call It Treason* series!

Who was behind allowing Red Chinese soldiers take airborne training at Fort Benning, Georgia?

Is this not treason?

Why was South Vietnam, South Africa, Rhodesia and numerous other American friends deliberately betrayed to the forces of evil?

Is this not treason?

Why was our friend Chiang Kai Shek not so gently coerced into a Communist dictatorship by highly placed subversives in the State Department?

Is this not treason?

Why was Cuba treasonously delivered into the clutches of Communist revolutionary Fidel Castro?

Is this not treason?

Why have untold millions of dollars consistently been used to prop up faltering Red dictatorships and to assist Communist terrorists in overthrowing non-Communist governments?

Is this not treason?

What American company sold nuclear reactors to Communist Occupied Romania?

Is this not treason?

Name the company that provided Communist Hungary with a factory designed to make 1.5 million light bulbs daily?

Is this not treason?

What well known oil company invested $1 billion for oil exploration in Communist Occupied Angola?

Is this not treason?

Can you name the American company who treasonously built and equipped a $10 million electronics plant near Warsaw for the Polish slave labor tyranny?

Is this not treason?

These are questions to which every American should rightfully have an honest answer.

Unfortunately most do not!

Tragedy was carefully orchestrated by traitors in our Government and the media with regard to Cuba, Vietnam, Laos, Cambodia, Rhodesia, China, El Salvador, Nicaragua and

many other countries.   Anastasio   Somoza
was the former President of free Nicaragua.

He offered this
startling insight in his 1980
book, Nicaragua Betrayed:
*"I have factual evidence that
the betrayal of Nicaragua
was not perpetrated out of
ignorance, but rather by
design."*

Somoza was soon after assassinated!

Is this not treason?

John Lehman, Secretary of the Navy,
made this shocking
statement on May 25 to the
1983 Annapolis graduating
class: *"Within weeks many
of you will be looking
across just hundreds of feet
of water at some of the most
modern technology ever invented in America.*

"Unfortunately, it is on
Soviet ships."

Is this not treason?

Earl E.T. Smith was the
American Ambassador to
Cuba when it was similarly
delivered to the Communists.

He makes this concise comment on July 14, 1986: *"Nicaragua is Cuba all over again."*

Can you name the company that paid the Communist dictatorship in Angola over $600 million annually in taxes and oil royalties.

This money bought new Soviet jets, tanks and helicopter gunships.

And it paid Castro for supplying 35,000 imported Cuban mercenaries who keep the Angolan people enslaved.

Is this not treason?

Stressed retired Brigadier General Andrew J. Gatsis on August 11, 1986: *"Though aware of the Communist goal of world domination, the average U.S. Citizen refuses to believe that the real threat comes from governmental officials and their non-governmental confederates who secretly espouse the same objectives as the openly avowed Communists."*

Anthony Sutton stated in his 1986 book *The Best Enemy Money Can Buy: "We now have the formidable task of bringing these gentlemen to the bar of justice to publicly answer for their private and*

concealed actions."

The *None Dare Call It Treason* series certainly won't win accolades from the United Nations or the State Department!

Nor will Harvard feel compelled to bestow an honorary degree upon the author!

Harvard Law School was the spawning ground for an incredible number of Red agents. Included were members of the first Soviet spy ring ever to be exposed in our government.

Reed Irvine aptly commented in July of 1986: *"Indeed, it has long been a joke among refugees from Eastern Europe that there are more Marxists at Harvard than there are in the Soviet Union, or Poland, or whatever Communist country the refugee called home."*

The Honorable Ezra Taft Benson said: *"The truth must be told even at the risk of*

23

destroying, in large measure, the influence of men who are widely respected and loved by the American people.

"The stakes are high. Freedom and survival is the issue."

Treason is still a most serious federal offense.

The *None Dare Call It Treason* series examines the reasons for and the Americans behind the fall of freedom and the rise of tyranny throughout the world!

**Has anything really changed?
You Decide!**

Treason

Whoever, owing allegiance to the United States, levies war against them or adheres to their enemies, giving them aid and comfort within the United States or elsewhere, is guilty of treason and shall suffer death, or be imprisoned not less than five years and fined not less than $10,000; and shall be incapable of holding any office under the United states.

U.S. Code, Title 18, Section 2381

Whoever, owing allegiance to the United States and having knowledge of the commission of any treason against them, conceals and does not, as soon as may be, disclose and make known the same to the President or to some judge of the United States, or to the Governor or to some judge or justice of a particular state, is guilty of misprision of treason, and shall be fined not more than $1000 or imprisoned not more than 7 years or both.

U.S. Code, Title 18, Section 2382

Treasonous Trade With and Aid to Enemies of Freedom

Treason: *". . . consciously and purposely acting to aid its [one's country] enemies."*

American Heritage Dictionary

"The Communist ideology is to destroy your society," charged Soviet exile Alexander Solzhenitsyn at the AFL/CIO dinner on July 30, 1975. *"This has never changed. When there is détente, peaceful co-existence, and trade, they will still insist: the ideological war must continue.*

"This is continued repetition of the oath to destroy the Western world. Just as, once upon a time in the Roman Senate, a famous speaker ended every speech with the statement: 'Furthermore, Carthage must be destroyed,' so today, with every act -- détente, trade, or whatever -- capitalism must be destroyed."

Vladimir Ilyich Lenin said: *"When the capitalist world starts to trade with us, on that day they will begin to finance their own destruction."*

And he also warned: *"Instead of using guns and tanks, we shall wage an industrial war.*

"As soon as we are strong enough to overthrow capitalism, we shall immediately seize it by the throat."

One government agency stealthily wheedles away untold tons of grain to Communist Occupied Russia and other enemy Red slave state dictatorships.

Shortages result and prices go up for Americans.

Farmers are unable to get enough grain to feed their livestock in order to produce meat.

Shortages again result!

Another government agency turns around and purchases its beef from Romania a Communist Occupied Country and enemy of the United States!

The billions of dollars in international giveaways is far more than just incredible!

It's uncontestably treason!

The amount of America's aid to and trade with Communist Bloc dictatorships who in time of war would march with the USSR is beyond comprehension.

That such mind boggling betrayal of trust had been allowed to take place or even condoned for so many years is incredible!

Even more alarming is the fact that all of America's leaders were aware of the pervasive perfidy continually taking place in Washington.

There appeared to be a *conspiracy of silence* regarding aid to and trade with Red enemies of the United States!

Past and present political leaders from the President on down had every reason to be fearful should the American citizenry ever obtain the untarnished facts.

Mikhail Makarenko spent eight long years in the Gulag Archipelago, This is Communist Occupied Russia's vast network of inhuman slave labor concentration camps.

He was asked how the barbaric Soviet regime could continue to stand after decades of such terrifying brutality and oppression.

His answer was *"Western trade."*

James J. Drummey charged on July 14, 1986: *"Human beings have been systematically tortured and murdered in the Soviet Union for more than 40 years.*

"More than 60,000,000 have perished in these camps.

"The murderers are now looking in your direction."

Made in the West media star Mikhail Sergeyvich Gorbachev is Lenin-Stalin-Khrushchev all rolled into one with the rough edges nicely polished and draped in an expensive made in the USA suit.

This violent Russian despite the drooling groveling and awed posturing struck by America's most influential leftist news, business and political luminaries came up through the murderous Communist ranks.

Gorbachev was really no more than a ruthless protégé of Yuri V. Andropov the violence prone monster who headed the feared KGB.

Marxist-Leninist dictators come and go with the passage of time. Nevertheless the inhumanity, barbarism and savagery always remain as a permanent fixture in the psyche of every Communist leader.

The West still aids and trades with these Marxist barbarians! We constantly do business with the most merciless enemy every faced by mankind.

Blatantly ignorant leftist politicians and Kremlin moles deeply imbedded in our government have long advocated unlimited trade with the USSR.

The idea of accelerated trade with America's deadly Communist adversary began to really bear fruit during the Administration of President John F. Kennedy. Washington subversives had more of a free hand to negotiate perfidious trade deals with the Soviets.

Secretary of Commerce Luther Hodges approved innumerable export licenses.

Ridiculous long-term, low and no-interest but high risk loans were freely granted to innumerable Communist dictatorships

Communist Occupied Russia's loans as well as all the others were guaranteed by the government.

The Soviets turned around and used this money to purchase American wheat, chemicals, computers, factories, etc.

The first attempt to justify such acts of treason was the 1960 *Ball Report.*

This rationalization was prepared under the direction of radical leftist George Ball (CFR) who was to become Kennedy's Under Secretary of State.

He lied reported the *New York Times* on January 8, 1962 when he declared that unlimited trade with Communist dictatorships was *"inevitable."*

Other early proponents of heavy trade in *strategic goods* with America's Red enemies were socialist Vice President Hubert H. Humphrey (CFR) and two other notorious security risks Secretary of State Dean Rusk and National Security Advisor Walt Rostow.

Former Congressman Martin Dies was for seven years Chairman of the House Committee on Un-American Activities. He said this about the liberal left in March of 1965: *"When the 'Liberals' are accused of having been 'soft' on Communism, they go into hysterics and scream that their accusers are 'unfair.'*

"The truth is that they have been soft on Communism from the very beginning, and they are still taking advantage of every opportunity to resume their policy of appeasing the Communists, whether it is by tacit approval of their  *physical crimes or by giving them reduced rates to buy our stores of foods and grains.*

"This is a sore spot with the 'Liberals,' but it is true with the majority of the 'Liberal' leaders that they continue to accommodate the Communist enemy at every opportunity.

"That, after all, is what being 'soft' on Communism is -- all about."

Six multinational grain dealers controlled all grain leaving the United States. They are Cargill, Andre, Bunge, Cook, Dreyfus and Continental.

Ninety percent of Continental Grain of New York was owned by the Fribourgs who were one of the world's wealthiest families.

When Jules Fribourg ran the company back in the 1930s he handled *millions of tons* of grain sales for the murderous Stalin regime.

The entire Russian grain crop had been confiscated from the peasant farmers. This was part of a diabolical plan of mass starvation devised and executed  by a Neanderthal monster known as Nikita Khrushchev.

Khrushchev's infamous famine was deliberately created from 1932-1935 as a direct result.

Roughly 14.5 million men, women and children were methodically starved to death in the Ukraine alone.

The Kennedy Administration wheat giveaways to Communist Occupied Russia in 1961 were beyond belief. These traitorous giveaways should have erupted into a national scandal!

But they didn't.

They hardly caused a ripple on the political scene.

Why?

Because the traitors carefully kept the public in the dark.

According to Congressman D.L. Latta on August 4, 1961: *"Officials of the U.S. Department of Agriculture and the Commerce Department agreed to sell surplus wheat to the Soviet Union for $.62 per bushel less than the baker who bakes your bread pays for it.*

"Some wheat shipped to the Soviets and their puppets is used to make ethyl alcohol.

"This in turn is used for manufacturing such war-related items as TNT, missile fuel, and poison gas!"

Treason?

Of course it was!

Communist Occupied Russia was sold $200 million worth of wheat in 1963.

Senator Thomas Dodd later noted on September 9, 1965: *"The wheat was not sold at the price which the government had paid the American farmer, but at the artificially low world price, so that the American government, in effect, was subsidizing the Soviet Union."*

Dodd pointed out at the time of the wheat deal that *"subsidized agricultural commodities should not be made available to the Soviet Union or to countries dominated by the USSR."*

"Sweetheart deals with the Reds are extensive and have been for decades," charged Joseph Mehrten. *"In fact, so extensive is this U.S. aid that without it Soviet leaders not only could not pursue expansionist policies but would be powerless and overthrown."*

Continental was instrumental in selling $78.5 million worth of American wheat to Communist Occupied Russia in 1964.

The Johnson Administration subsidized $24 million of this package!

This was almost one-third the cost!

Treason?

Of course it was!

Such a sweetheart deal enabled the USSR to purchase U.S. wheat at a price lower than could friendly nations.

Cargill of Minneapolis sold $53 million worth of U.S. wheat to the same Soviet murderers.

Treason?

What else could this possible be?

American taxpayer's again subsidized the sale!

This time for $18 million.

In just a little more than a month in 1964 more than 65 million bushels of subsidized wheat was shipped to the Soviet slave empire.

Even more treason?

Certainly!

This was enough wheat to give a bushel to every third man, woman and child in the USSR revealed a March 1964 statement issued by the Department of Agriculture.

 According to former Secretary of Agriculture Ezra Taft Benson it cost taxpayers $42 million to subsidize this grain giveaway to our Communist *"friends."*

In the meantime, Communist Occupied Russia shipped tons of subsidized American wheat to Cuba, Romania and other satellite dictatorships!

This was done in order to strengthen the USSR's grip on these Captive Nations.

On the other hand American grains and other food commodities were being traded or given away to some non-Communist nations.

They in turn shipped them to the Reds!

 For example in 1964 Nasser received *$1 billion* in grains and other agricultural products from the United States.

The Egyptian government turned around and shipped 314,000 tons of these food commodities to Communist Occupied

Russia, East Germany, Romania, China, Hungary, Cuba and Bulgaria!

Brazil pulled a similar stunt when in 1965 they were given $61 million worth of free food commodities.

The appreciative Brazilian government using Russian freighters sent eight thousand tons of American corn to Communist Occupied Cuba!

The USSR is unquestionably history's largest food importer.

Even in its best years the Soviets produce far less food than does the United States.

This is accomplished with 50 percent more land under cultivation and an incredible 1,000 percent more farm workers.

Here's an interesting point to consider: Approximately three percent of the U.S. labor force farms yet vast surpluses are continually produced.

In Communist Occupied Russia around 25 percent or one-fourth of the work force farms.

Despite this they're still unable to produce enough food to feed their own people.

Charles R. Armour noted in 1986: *"The premise that the Soviet Union is feeding its people, supporting its utopian society, creating its industrial, technological, and military capabilities as a socialistic state is the height of absurdity."*

1971 was another banner year for Americans supplying food to feed the Red Army!

On November 5, the Department of Agriculture announced that Cargill and Continental Grain would sell another $136 million worth of heavily subsidized oats and barley to the USSR.

The Russians purchased them for less than half price. This was certainly quite a bargain for an avowed enemy of the seller!

During the summer of 1972 identified Soviet espionage agent Henry *"Bor"* Kissinger and his old leftist friend Helmut Sonnenfeldt pushed hard to *"sell"* Communist Occupied Russia *400 million* more bushels of American wheat.

Sonnenfeldt had been exposed as a Kremlin mole. He was a serious security risk who'd long been under investigation for spying.

In fact the FBI recommended that he be prosecuted under existing espionage statutes.

He never was!

Why?

Prices on this *Great Grain Robbery* were deliberately kept low.

Some $300 million in subsidies were paid by our government to the exporting companies.

The long-standing *Needy Russian-Welfare-Program* was still in full swing!

Comrades in Washington gave their comrades in Moscow another *$1 billion* worth of American wheat at unheard of bargain-basement prices!

The Commodity Credit Corporation *"loaned"* Communist Occupied Russia $760 million at 6-1/8 percent so they could pay for the wheat they were stealing!

Treasury had actually paid a higher interest rate to borrow the money than was charged to the ever needy Soviets.

American taxpayers were forced to guarantee the $750 million Soviet loan.

The Nixon Administration even agreed to deliver one-third of the Russian booty to Odessa at American expense.

Incredible but true nonetheless!

Treason once again?

What else could this be called?

U.S. shippers were paid a special subsidy of $12.95 per ton or a total of around $80 million in this segment of the notorious *Aid-to-Dependent-Communists-Program.*

Such treasonous grain transactions raised domestic prices of wheat from $1.63 to almost $4.50 per bushel.

The Russians obtained incredible amounts of barley, rye, corn, oats, sorghum, soybeans and approximately one-third of America's entire wheat crop.

Food prices skyrocketed in the United States during the early 1970s!

This was a direct result of the illegal commodity giveaways to Communist

Occupied Russia and the Red Bloc dictatorships.

Taxpayers were subsidizing bread at 11 cents a pound for Moscow housewives.

The *New York Times* reported: *"While [American] housewives are paying higher prices, Russian bread remains one of the biggest bargains in the Soviet Union."*

The Great Grain Robbery also forced a scandalous jump in meat prices. $1.5 billion was added to the cost of meat purchased by American consumers.

This was a direct result of grain shortages which brought on the exorbitant cost of grain needed to feed livestock.

Despite all this the criminal food giveaways continued.

Washington correspondent Paul Scott exposed the next facet of Nixon's *Needy-Russian-Welfare-Program*: *"A massive new food and grain deal provides for Russia obtaining U.S. food for virtually nothing.*

45

"Russia would pay for the grain in its own currency [worthless outside of Russia] which would have to be used on projects within the Soviet Union."

Leonid Brezhnev was Moscow's answer to Howdy Doody.

This decrepit dictator told the Soviet Politburo and the Warsaw Pact dictators in 1973: *"We Communists have got to string along with the capitalists for a while.*

"We need their agriculture and their technology.

"But we are going to continue massive military programs and by the middle 80's we will be in a position to return to a much more aggressive foreign policy designed to gain the upper hand in our relationship with the West."

In his first 1981 Presidential news conference Ronald Reagan said: *"I know of no leader of the Soviet Union since the revolution, and including the present leadership, that has not more than once repeated in the various Communist congresses that their goal must be the promotion of world revolution and a one-world socialist or Communist state."*

Despite such rhetoric the *New York Times* noted: *"The United States has agreed to nearly triple -- to 23 million metric tons -- the amount of American wheat and corn that the Soviet Union will be allowed to purchase in the next 12 months.*

"The agreement set the stage for record purchases of American grain."

Secretary of Agriculture John Block was fully aware of slave labor usage on Russia's Siberian pipeline.

Yet this traitor gave the Kremlin a new five year contract for subsidized bargain-basement priced American grain in 1982.

In this way Block guaranteed the Red Army and the concentration camp guards wouldn't go without food.

How harmless to American security are such massive grain giveaways to the USSR?

Russian General Yevdokin Yegorovich Maltsev quoted Lenin: *"The Red Army cannot be strong without great state reserves of wheat because without this the army cannot be moved about freely, nor trained as it should be.*

"Without this one cannot maintain the workers who work for the army."

Soviet exile Mikhail Makarenko warned in a 1981 Heritage Foundation monograph: *"Grain bought from the West is earmarked for the Soviet armed forces, not the people."*

How did the Soviets thank the United States?

They brazenly assassinated or captured Congressman Lawrence McDonald and massacred or took prisoner 60 other Americans in the September 1, 1983, terrorist attack on Korean Airlines Flight 007.

A missile fired from a Soviet fighter struck one of the Boeing 747's four engines.

The national media reported that the Japanese Civil Aviation Bureau *"confirmed that the Hokkaido radar followed Air Korea to a landing in Soviet territory on the island of*

Sakhalin" where all 269 passengers and crew were safe.

By the next day it was being reported around the world that KAL 007 had been blown out of the sky.

The Russians claimed it was a spy plane flying over the highly restricted Kamchatka peninsula.

This the Russians claimed was the site of the Petropavlovsk naval port where 90 nuclear submarines were based along with 30 land based ballistic missiles aimed at the United States.

The area was so sensitive that the Soviets claimed six colonels had been executed for failing to destroy U.S. planes crossing the region.

Georgia Representative Larry McDonald was on the flight!

He was a staunch anticommunist who was the new president of the John Birch Society.

McDonald was making the trip to Korea to help memorialize the 30th anniversary of the official U.S. entry into the Korean War.

He was to meet a congressional delegation in Seoul led by Senator Jesse Helms and Senator Steve Symms.

Fortunately both men decided at the last

minute to take another flight while Senator Orrin Hatch arrived on a flight from China.

Communist Occupied Russia was given another gift two days before Christmas 1985.

Reagan's new Farm Bill created yet another loathsome grain giveaway program!

A major portion of American wheat, corn and other farm products worth $2 billion went to Dictator Mikhail Gorbachev's Soviet Union.

August 1, 1986, saw a brand new facet of America's perfidious *Communist Welfare Program* at work.

The Reagan Administration announced the most bizarre wheat deal to date.

America's *"friends"* in Moscow were offered $52 million worth of free grain!

This gift was supposed to induce

Gorbachev's Red tyranny to purchase more wheat from the U.S. at the going world price.

Called *"export enhancement,"* it was simply a phrase used to camouflage the donating of more subsidized wheat to the sanguinary Soviet adversary.

In other words American taxpayers whether they liked it or not would actually *pay* the Russian gangsters to take U.S. wheat surpluses off our hands!

Wheat to feed their military!

Wheat to send to Communist Occupied Cuba or Ethiopia or Hungary!

These same Soviet *"friends"* who feed their military with wheat and other farm products donated by the United States are taking special precautions for the war they considered to be inevitable!

Russia's Communist Party bosses including Dictator Gorbachev have carefully planned the assassination of every important American leader.

This was to be undertaken by Spetsnaz or Special Purpose troops.

These are elite commando units or Special Purpose troops who have been highly trained to successfully carry out their murderous assignment.

Intelligence groups know of a great many Spetsnaz teams already in place throughout the United States.

Our government has made a concerted effort to keep this under wraps.

"Why has America built the world's most modern, most highly automated steel finishing plant for the Communist government of Poland?" asked the *Dallas Morning News* on July 13, 1961. *"Constructed in Warren, Ohio, the plant was dedicated as the Lenin Steel Works.*

"The American people 'lent' the Communists $2.5 million to pay for it."

Strategic trade with Communist satellite nations started zooming upwards during the Kennedy White House years.

Business leaders were pressured to get on the Red trade bandwagon.

The *Baltimore Sun* reported on December 14, 1962: *"The government is quietly encouraging American businessmen to expand their trade with the Soviet bloc."*

Eight million tons of scrap iron were loaded in Houston, Texas, revealed Congressman John Ashbrook on August 31, 1961.

The destination?

Communist Occupied Czechoslovakia!

At the same time, scrap iron and steel worth $700,000 were shipped to Communist Occupied Yugoslavia!

Treason?

Of course!

"Non-strategic" railroad equipment valued at around $2.5 million went to Communist Occupied Bulgaria.

Treason?

Absolutely1

What else could this be called?

All these things were taking place during the 1961 Berlin crisis when Nikita

Khrushchev ordered the construction of the infamous Berlin wall. Communist Occupied Russia effectively sealed off East Berlin and stopped the massive exodus of enslaved citizens.

Khruschev gave a speech on June 19, 1962, in Bucharest, Romania.

This depraved mass-murdering beast boasted: *"The United States will eventually fly the Communist flag. The American people will hoist it themselves!"*

In February 1963 the State Department announced that Communist Occupied Poland was getting $51.6 million worth of surplus farm products on long-term credit.

This was to eventually be paid to the U.S. in worthless Polish zlotys.

These zlotys could be spent only in Poland!

At this particular time American trade with Poland totaled $477.3 million.

Such deals could be expected from the State Department while Dean Rusk was in charge.

Rusk was never identified as a Communist mole but he was an extremely serious security risk nevertheless.

His never varying pro-Red track record speaks for itself!

The Senate Judiciary Committee thoroughly investigated trade between the

United States and Communist slave labor dictatorships in 1964.

It actually took a Senate investigation to determine that American-Red Bloc trade wasn't conducive to the well being of our nation!

The Senate report stated: *"On the Communist side East-West trade is a matter of survival.*

"The Communist bloc must have Western assistance not only in coping with its chronic agricultural crises, but also to cope with the chronic deficiencies of its industries."

Tom Anderson was absolutely correct in January of 1975 when he said: *"The very survival of the Communist World rests upon the willingness and production of the Free World to support it."*

Congressman Ed Derwinski charged on July 1, 1975: *"It is not the intention of the [Johnson] administration merely to permit expanded trade agreements with Communist governments, but it is their specific intention to subsidize that trade."*

During the Vietnam War a phenomenal portion of

America's national treasure was generously dumped on 99 different countries.

The majority of the greedy recipients of America's *International Welfare Program* either claimed to be neutral.

Or they openly sided with Communist Occupied North Vietnam!

This certainly doesn't speak well for the common sense quotient of the leftists permeating various echelons of our government.

These *"misguided"* bureaucrats always excuse such traitorous giveaways with the illogical reasoning that America is buying the loyalty of these so-called *"friends."*

The Johnson Administration treasonously aided Todor Zhivkov's Communist Occupied Bulgaria.

It sanctioned the giveaway of a factory for making platinum pellets.

These special pellets are required for making high octane gasoline.

The Reds actually paid nothing although the cost was $166 million dollars!

The Soviet puppet was given long-term credit for the purchase as all Marxist-Leninist dictatorships have come to expect from America.

Why does the U.S. do anything to aid this Bulgarian tyranny?

After all it was commonly known to be run by one of the harshest and most pervasive secret police organizations in the entire Russian Bloc!

Insanity or outright treason is evident when the United States enthusiastically transfers its most modern technology to Communist Occupied Russia and its Red slave state clones.

These are the international Al Capones.

These are the tyrants behind the murderous terrorist activities in the West.

They're the same Communist criminals who organized the anti-war (actually anti-U.S. -- pro-Hanoi) movements during the Vietnam era.

They're the same revolutionary gangsters who were behind the no-win Vietnam War itself!

They're the ones orchestrating the anti U.S. -- pro-Soviet peace at any price movement today.

And they're the ideological brothers of the zealots who coldly disemboweled pregnant women!

Bayoneted helpless babies!

And blew the hands and feet off little children with booby trapped toys in Afghanistan and elsewhere around the world!

During his 1968 campaign Richard Nixon self-righteously protested the Johnson Administration's treasonous trade policies with Communist Occupied Russia and other satellite Red dictatorships.

Once in office Nixon did an about face and advocated even more trade.

He substantially increased the giveaway of strategic war supplies to these enemy nations.

They in turn shipped arms, ammunition, and other war goods to Communist Occupied North Vietnam to be used in slaughtering American troops.

The Nixon Administration further opened the trade floodgates in 1973.

Restrictions were treasonously ignored regarding shipments to Communist countries for an incredible *"350 types of electronic instruments, machinery, transport equipment, 470 chemicals and 300 classes of metals and metal products."*

In 1971, over 1,800 more *"restricted"* items were deleted from the list of non-tradable goods.

 In 1974, Richard Nixon allowed huge quantities of low sulphur coal to be shipped to both Communist Occupied Yugoslavia and Communist Occupied Romania.

Such clean burning coal was delivered to America's enemies despite the fact that it was desperately needed by the U.S. steel industry!

As a direct result many Americans found themselves out of work.

Syndicated columnist Victor Riesel had this to say in May of 1974: *"So acute is Bethlehem Steel's need for this low sulphur coal, it is cutting back 'hot metal' production by a million tons in the next six months . . . the U.S. steel industry lies under a pall.*

"Few have more than dangerously short supplies of this special coal."

In 1981 Communist Occupied Romania became Eastern Europe's biggest market for American exports.

As could be expected Romania purchased all of these American goodies on credit.

This is but another ingenious leftist method of giving one more Red enemy foreign aid through the back door.

The United States gave aid to and traded with the Red dictatorship in Romania despite the fact that Nicolae Ceausescu vehemently finds any degree of free enterprise *"incompatible with socialism."*

Ambassador Zdzislaw M. Ruraz defected to the United States when Polish dictator General Wojciech Jaruzelski declared martial law in 1981.

Ruraz offered his expert view on East-West trade in March of 1986: *"I know how absolutely essential trade with the West is to the Communist bloc.*

"Without it they could not sustain their economies and they certainly could not continue to support the Soviet armaments build up that now threatens the entire world."

Soviet *advisors"* and 20,000 Cuban soldiers were brought to Communist Occupied Ethiopia in 1978.

More than 5,000 students were savagely butchered in February of 1978 alone.

Some as young as 12 years old were according to Jeanne Kirkpatrick (CFR) *"immersed in hot oil, sexually tortured, or flung out of windows and left to die in the streets."*

During 1984 the same kinds of atrocities were still taking place!

American leaders treasonously delivered more than 41 metric tons of food to the Ethiopian Red despots.

The cost came to $22.7 million.

During 1985 the United States donated another $127 million worth of humanitarian aid to hapless Ethiopia.

Included were 223,000 metric tons of food.

A ridiculous $12.40 per ton *import tax* was charged by the Marxist-Leninist dictatorship on *all* the food unloaded from American ships.

Mind you this was food donated to help alleviate the suffering caused by the despotic regimes planned famine program!

The murderous Ethiopian leadership made it clear!

They were intentionally starving certain

 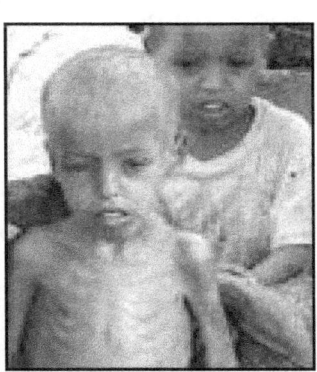

segments of their population.

Despite this on November 2, 1984 the U.S. and Ethiopia agreed to yet another treasonous government-to-government humanitarian assistance program under which the U.S. provided 50,000 metric tons of food directly to the Ethiopian Government.

This was all reported in a little noticed January 1985 State Department briefing paper.

Solzhenitsyn warned on November 25 1981 that U.S. leaders are making the same errors with Communist Occupied China that were previously made with the Soviet gangsters:

"In 30 or 40 years you will read about he Chinese Gulag and you will be stunned, you will say, well, we didn't know; but you must know today what's going on.

"By trusting China you will yield the other half of the earth.

"They're the same Communists, they use the same methods, and they use the annihilation policy."

The diabolical scheme of supplying food commodities to America's Red Chinese adversary goes back many years.

The administrative chief of the United States UN delegation was a notorious Kremlin mole named Louis Bohmrich. This Soviet spy advocated a traitorous *Marshall Plan* for Communist Occupied China in 1966.

This radical leftist was quoted in the *Indianapolis News* on January 11, 1966: *"Every effort must be made to help China evolve.*

'We must guarantee that China does not have to fight for food. It must be assured."

One simple question for all of the above!

Why?

Because of a deeply planted Soviet mole who was in a position to make such treasonous decisions.

Various Communist occupied countries had long been profitably looting the American food supply.

The *Los Angeles Herald Examiner* revealed on July 27, 1973: *"Congressional conferees Thursday tentatively agreed to authorize low-interest, long-term credit sales of food to Russia, China, Cuba, and other Communist countries. "Repayment under such deals can extend 20 years with interest rates as low as 2 percent."*

Was your Congressman a part of this treasonous activity?

It can easily be said that the whole world dines at America's table.

The trouble is that the United States always gets stuck with the check.

American citizens pay cash for their food yet atheistic Communist dictatorships get theirs for virtually nothing.

According to correspondent Paul Scott in May of 1974: *"Members of Congress and the nation's farm leaders are being privately told that if the Nixon Administration has its way, there will be no reversal of this policy of furnishing cut-rate and free food to Moscow and Peking."*

Whose side was Richard Nixon and his leftist cohorts on anyway?

How can the United States spend $300 billion a year to defend itself against Communist aggression while it's also feeding the Communist aggressors?

There certainly was no reversal in Nixon's *International Red Welfare Policy*!

A news dispatch from Hong Kong on August 22, 1973 revealed the astounding amounts of three major food items Communist Occupied China was allowed to *"purchase"* from the U.S. on credit.

These freebies were:

Corn -- 630,000 metric tons.

Wheat -- almost 127 million bushels.

Soybeans -- 950,000 metric tons.

Soybean shipments to Japan who was a paying customer and an ally had to be embargoed in order to fill Mao's demands.

Over and above these food commodities this deadly dictatorship was given 775,000 bales of surplus subsidized cotton.

According to the *Kansas City Times* of August 21, 1973 this *"equaled the amount of cotton exported"* to all nations in 1972.

And it tripled the price of cotton in the United States!

Communist Occupied China's Three Gorges Dam on the Yangtze River is the biggest in the world.

Amazingly enough Reagan's Department of the Interior helped the despicable Red dictatorship build this 13 million kilowatt hydroelectric facility.

It was originally designed for Chiang Kai-shek's Free China.

This was undertaken by engineers in the Interior Department's Reclamation Bureau back during World War II.

According to the *New York Times* on August 28, 1973 the Three Gorges Dam project had been shelved in 1947 when Mao's *"agrarian reformers"* were instigating insurrection and terrorizing the countryside in an effort to violently communize the country.

So impassioned was America's love affair with the murderous Red Chinese regime that trade blossomed to a new high of $8.1 billion in 1985.

The United States exported $3.9 billion worth of goods to Red China!

Included were computers, ammunition factories and high-tech machinery.

In return, the Chinese slave-masters sent America $4.2 billion worth of merchandise including:

  fire crackers
  honey
  cheap clothing
  straw hats
  Christmas tree ornaments
  wicker baskets
  dolls
  stuffed toys
  alarm clocks, etc.

None of these things were vital to national security or the U.S. economy.

There's no question but that such trade practices directly aided and abetted Communist Occupied China in the barbaric suppression of her enslaved people.

Senator Richard G. Lugar chairman of the Foreign Relations Committee illogically commented on June 2, 1986: *"I believe ultimately it is in our interests to cooperate with China and I am convinced that this does not disrupt the current military balance between*  *the People's Republic of China and Taiwan."*

Garbage!

President Reagan's Treasury Secretary James Baker paid a visit to Red China.

While in Peking, he was quoted on June 2, 1986 as saying the Administration was *"eager to help China move forward to modernize and develop its economy in whatever way is mutually acceptable."*

Did Baker not know that the diabolical Communist military ordered their men to decapitate political leaders, impale their heads on wooden posts, and place the posts on all roads coming into a village?

Or did he even care?

Did Baker not know that the diabolical Communist military allowed their men to massacre mothers and their children with flame throwers?

Or did he even care?

Did Baker not know that the diabolical Communist military ordered their men to to bury people alive in ant hills?

Or did he even care?

Did Baker not know that the diabolical Communist military commonly made a practice of executing American POWs after tightly wiring their hands behind their backs?

Or did he even care?

In 1985 China's Communist Party Chief Hu Yau-bang claimed his country wasn't strong enough militarily to attack Free China (Taiwan).

He said Red China could make such a move in four to eight years.

Yau-bang was quoted on October 13, 1986: *"We have to wait until our economy is on the right track. Military power is economic power."*

Lugar, Baker and many others evidently need to be reminded of a few pertinent facts about Communist Occupied China.

Whole classes of people are thrown into medieval prisons and left to rot.

Others are starved to death; summarily executed; tortured; or incarcerated in one of the thousands of disease-infested slave labor camps.

Dr. David Rowe, Far Eastern specialist at Yale explained: *"Perhaps the most pervasive illusion underlying the U.S. China policy is the belief that as of today Communist China has substantially changed.*

"So Mao is dead, like Stalin, but have Teng Hsiao-ping and his clique abandoned Marxism?

"Have they abandoned their basic war against capitalism?

"To both these questions we must answer with a resounding no."

"The liberals hope you'll believe them when they tell you how anti-Communist they are," declared Ezra Taft Benson in his 1964 book *Principles and National Survival*. *"But they become alarmed if you really inform yourself on the subject of Socialistic-Communism.*

"For after you inform yourself, you might begin to study the liberal voting record.

"And this study would show you how much the liberals are giving aid and comfort to the enemy and how much the liberals are actually leading America towards socialism itself.

"Communism is just another form of Socialism, as is Fascism."

Vice Premier Yao Yi-lin of the Communist Chinese State Council made an official pilgrimage to the Soviet Union in July 1985.

Yao was the most important Chinese official to visit Moscow in 20 years.

At this time, America's new found Chinese *"friends"* signed a $14 billion agreement with their Russian *"enemy."*

Peking agreed to sell the Soviets raw materials, agricultural products, and various consumer products.

Communist Occupied Russia would update 17 Chinese industrial plants and build them seven new factories.

This certainly doesn't sound very antagonistic!

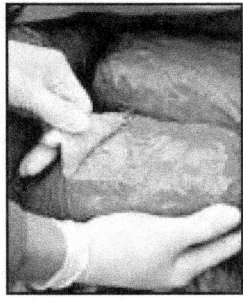

It's worth reminding American leaders from the President on down about Communist Occupied China's heavy involvement in the illegal drug trade.

Intelligence specialist Frank Capell revealed in January of 1974: *"Red China's trade in narcotics has grown to more than double her official foreign trade, amounting to about $15 billion a year.*

"70 percent of the heroin in the United States comes from Red China. The U.S. Government has tried to suppress this fact."

The Red Chinese dictatorship according to leftist American leaders should be sold nuclear technology.

Their reasoning?

Communist Occupied China can be used as a counter balance to the military might of Communist Occupied Russia.

Surely they must have been kidding!

Distinguished Senator Barry Goldwater vehemently disagreed on April 21, 1986: *"This ignores the insistence of Peking that it is not an 'ally' of the United States, and the argument is blind to the growing accommodation between the Communist giants."*

On July 23, 1985 President Ronald Reagan and Communist Occupied China's dictator Li Ziannian signed a nuclear accord.

This agreement opened the door to the giveaway of more of America's highly guarded nuclear technology!

Red China estimates it will have at least 10 American nuclear power plants operating by the year 2000.

Thank you President Reagan!

Less than one year later in March 1986 the Chinese-Russian *"growing accommodation"* noted by Goldwater surfaced more clearly.

Red China's Vice Premier Li Peng announced that the two dictatorships would exchange nuclear technicians and engineers.

On April 3, it was further revealed that nuclear power plants in Communist Occupied Russia were to be studied by Chinese nuclear experts.

These two slave labor tyrannies also agreed to more closely cooperate in coordinating their state-planned economies.

W.F. Rockwell Jr. was Chairman of the Board of North American Rockwell.

This man stood out as a beacon of ethics in the greed-filled corporate community.

He declared: *"I don't agree that trade is feasible, as long as we are faced with fighting the Communist-Bloc countries.*

"I dislike losing business to foreign countries; however at the same time I hesitate selling materials to any country which eventually might prove to be instrumental in killing U.S. troops."

Was this not a wonderful breath of fresh air?

Epilogue

The record covering crucial episodes of the McCarthy era has been massively and deliberately distorted from the very beginning!

Conveniently forgotten or deliberately overlooked are the 78 hearings held between 1951 and 1952 by Senator William E. Jenner's (R-Indiana) Senate Internal Security Subcommittee (SISS); the House Committee On Internal Security; the House Un-American Activities Committee (HUAC) under the chairmanship of both Martin Dies (D-Texas) and Francis Walters (D-Pa); the Federal Bureau of Investigation (FBI) under the guidance of J. Edgar Hoover; and other investigating committees and individuals.

Out of all of these investigations one man was selected:

To be stopped!

To be destroyed!

To be made an example!

Why?

So that no one would ever again dare to initiate any investigations into the penetration of our government agencies by communist agents (spies) in the employ of the Soviet Union!

Yes!

An obscure Senator from Wisconsin was deliberately targeted for this purpose!

Joseph McCarthy's incredibly successful investigations panicked those on the political left.

Their reaction was shockingly quick!

Key data was been suppressed, denied and even widely falsified.

This took place in the media, all branches of government and many alleged scholars entrenched in the ivory towers of our institutions of higher learning!

Such misreporting and misrepresentation of the facts continues today.

Much of the misinformation we were (and still are today) so carefully spoon-fed about Senator Joseph McCarthy the man and his investigations was no more than an admixture of uncheckable blovations from deceased third parties and demonstratable falsehoods!

For example, how many innocent people were harmed by McCarthy's revelations?

The correct answer?

Not one!

No!

Not One!

McCarthy's most virulent critics have had more than a half century to produce the names of the hundreds of innocent people they claim were destroyed by the astounding revelations of the Senator from Wisconsin.

Yet those highly skilled propagandists in our media and government and institutions of higher learning have been unable to name even one innocent person they claim was destroyed after being falsely accused by McCarthy!

How many innocent people committed suicide as a result of McCarthy's exposure?

The correct answer?

Not one!

Not one suicide can be attributed to the investigations conducted by McCarthy!

No! Not one!

According to the obscene claims made the highly skilled propagandists in our media, government and scholars entranced in those ivory towers of our colleges and universities there were a rash of suicides with bodies falling constantly of the heads of pedestrians below on the streets of Manhattan!

Once again, McCarthy's most virulent critics have had more than 50 years to produce the names of the hundreds of innocent people they claim committed suicide because of the astounding revelations of the Senator from Wisconsin.

Yet those highly skilled propagandists in our media and government and institutions of higher learning have been unable to name even one innocent person they claim committed suicide after being falsely accused by McCarthy!

No!

Not one!

But there were two suicides on record during the McCarthy period!

Neither was the result of an innocent person who'd been ruined by McCarthy's revelations!

Both were subversives who'd been exposed by McCarthy!

Both were subversives who'd been positively indentified as Kremlin agents!

Lawrence Duggan had been operating in the State Department as a widely known Soviet spy!

He'd been called to testify before a Congressional investigating committee.

Duggan never made it!

He conveniently "fell" from a window high up in a Manhattan skyscraper!

Fell?

Probably not!

He was more than likely pushed from or tossed out of the window by an assassin in the employ of the Soviet Union!

Why?

To make certain he didn't fold under pressure and start naming other Kremlin moles.

Secondly there was the unexpected demise of Harry Dexter White.

This Soviet agent discovered that he was being investigated by J. Edgar Hoover of the FBI!

He died of a sudden heart attack!

Coincidence?

Not hardly!

Was White's death a suicide?

Yes or at least so claimed McCarthy's critics!

Again, not hardly!

Heart attacks can readily be induced with the proper use of certain medicines administered by a hired assassin in the employ of the Kremlin!

Why?

Simply to eliminate anyone who might panic and decide to turncoat and reveal the names of other spies secretly entrenched deeply in the bowels of every branch of our government.

To sum up, most fit into one of three categories:

Conscience lacking incurable liars!

Those with an axe to grind!

Individuals who simply do not know the facts!

If you liked this book in the *None Dare Call It Treason* series then you'll probably also enjoy reading the others!

Gift copies of this book can be ordered at createspace.com/4216873

Available Titles

None Dare Call It Treason Book 1
The Internal Security Farce!
5.5" x 8.5" 97 pages $4.95
Order from createspace.com/4215951

None Dare Call It Treason Book 2
Never Ending Subversion
In Government!
5.5" x 8.5" 202 pages $4.95
Order from createspace.com/4216385

None Dare Call It Treason Book 3
America's Subversive State Department
Bloated With Security Risks
5.5" x 8.5" 202 pages $4.95
Order from createspace.com/4216626

None Dare Call It Treason Book 4
America's Illustrious State Department!
It's Machiavellian Misdeeds!
5.5" x 8.5" 202 pages $4.95
Order from createspace.com/4215018

None Dare Call It Treason Book 5
Our Presidents A Major Security Threat!
5.5" x 8.5" 202 pages $4.95
Order from createspace.com/4213501

None Dare Call It Treason Book 6
Presidential Words & Deeds
&Blatant Lies!
5.5" x 8.5" 202 pages $4.95
Order from createspace.com/4213920

None Dare Call It Treason Book 7
Subversives Close To Our Presidents
5.5" x 8.5" 89 pages $4.95
Order from createspace.com/4213931

None Dare Call It Treason Book 8
Henry Kissinger
The Shadowy Untouchable Kremlin Spy!
5.5" x 8.5" 202 pages $4.95

Order from createspace.com/4214986

None Dare Call It Treason Book 9
Inexcusably Arming America's Enemies!
5.5" x 8.5" 202 pages $4.95
Order from createspace.com/4216634

None Dare Call It Treason Book 10
Inexcusably Financing
America's Enemies!
5.5" x 8.5" 202 pages $4.95
Order from createspace.com/4216777

None Dare Call It Treason Book 11
Treasonous   Trade With & Aid To
Enemies Of Freedom!
5.5" x 8.5" 202 pages $4.95
Order from createspace.com/4216873

None Dare Call It Treason Book 12
Wholesale Treason During the War
In Vietnam!
5.5" x 8.5" 202 pages $4.95
Order from createspace.com/4215293

None Dare Call It Treason Book 13

Big Business
& Astounding Acts Of Treason!
5.5" x 8.5" 202 pages $4.95
Order from createspace.com/4215805

None Dare Call It Treason Book 14
Illegally Importing
Slave Made Goodies!
5.5" x 8.5" 202 pages $4.95
Order from createspace.com/4215894

None Dare Call It Treason Book 15
The House That Hiss Built
The Anti-American United Nations!
5.5" x 8.5" 202 pages $4.95
Order from createspace.com/4215323

None Dare Call It Treason Book 16
Security Risks in the House and Senate!
5.5" x 8.5" 202 pages $4.95
Order from createspace.com/4213508

None Dare Call It Treason Book 17
The Supreme Court A Devastating
Threat To National Security!

5.5" x 8.5" 202 pages $4.95
Order from createspace.com/4213699

None Dare Call It Treason Book 18
The Supreme Court and Congress
Devastating Threats
To National Security!
5.5" x 8.5" 202 pages $9.95
Order from createspace.com/

None Dare Call It Treason Book 19
Our Presidents
A Threat to National Security!
5.5" x 8.5" 202 pages $4.95
Order from createspace.com/

None Dare Call It Treason Book 20
Subversives Close To Our Presidents
5.5" x 8.5" 202 pages $4.95
Order from createspace.com/

None Dare Call It Treason Book 21
America's Subversive
State Department
5.5" x 8.5" 202 pages $4.95
Order from createspace.com/

None Dare Call It Treason Book 22
Never Ending Subversion
In Government
5.5" x 8.5" 202 pages $4.95
Order from createspace.com/

Orders for Resale
40% Off Retail Price

Send Purchase Order to

christianamerica2@yahoo.com

MEET
THE AUTHOR

Robert W. Pelton has been writing for more than 45 years on political and historical subjects.

He has published more than 100 books including the sensational *Unwanted Dead or Alive – The Greatest Act of Treason in Our History*

Mr. Pelton proudly claims a heritage going all the way back to well before the War for American Independence.

One of his ancestors, John Rogers, came to America on the Mayflower and was one of 41 signers of the Mayflower Compact.

Another, John Smith was one of the founders of Jamestown.

Peleg Pelton served as the fifer in the Continental Army at age 17 during the Battle of Saratoga (1777) and again in Yorktown (1781).

Captain Peter Hager was Commander of the Old Stone Fort in Schoharie, New York, in 1780.

Mr. Pelton is a member of Sons of the Revolution (SOR), and Sons of the American Revolution (SAR).